LIMBOLANDS

D1610537

For my family -
Rockstone and Starlight
Shine on!

Plateaux

Chakari scratching like a wild cat
spitting. hissing
all nails, teeth and wild hair
Old Cora nods in the doorway.
Ah yes, it is so
It is so.

LIMBOLANDS

Poems
by
Maggie Harris

MANGO PUBLISHING
1999

First published 1999

Published by Mango Publishing, London UK
P.O. Box 13378, London SE27 OZN

ISBN 1 902294 09 2

British Library Cataloguing in Publication Data
A CIP catalogue record for this book is available from the British Library

Printed in the UK by Intype Ltd, Wimbledon

Cover photograph and cover design by Maggie Harris

CONTENTS

I/SLANDS

LIMBO/LANDS

The Limbo Walkers

I sit with my father by the river
He is dead, we both know that
The Berbice River wets his feet, not mine.

I point my fingers to the far bank
A line of travellers wait
The Berbice waters move to greet them.

    Some have already braved her
    They stride mid-channel
    Growing taller
    Disbelief dissolving with each step.

I turn my face from river to daddy
He answers me with liquid eyes:
Those are the Limbo Walkers.

The Musician

He left it behind when they took him
His ankles forced into the same iron
His arms twisted behind his back

Others stumbled beside him
Tethered the same
Their pace forced by those who smelt of the sea

The musician uttered a long frightened howling
Almost close to the songs Tsaba had sung at sundown
Beside him, and part of him
His chains echoed an eerie accompaniment.

Abandoned Stations

Apart
　　from sitting in railway stations
generations later
　　swapping her silver for a stool
Boadicea
　　she of herstory making, vaguely remembered
charioteering
　　 in spaces where the leylines ran
　　crossing energies underground

She'd crossed
　　the tracks of memory
To this place
　　where the pylons grew
Taller
　　than the men she threw,
Where
　　sleepers and overhead lines ran on
　　shivering in the shock of life

She'd paused
　　like travellers do, to recharge
Seeking
　　the mains adaptor
Was caught
　　like travellers are in that space
Where
　　comfort is mistaken for identity
　　and energies play tic tac toe

Now
>her true blue cool blue sweeps the runners

Using up
>their lives as fast as the track

Runs along
>their singular view. And icons and pylons

and railway sleepers
>suck and stifle and recycle the cries
>howling through abandoned stations.

Lord of the Dance

I'll never see Nureyev dance now
even this poor attempt at an accolade
may not be meant for him
but for that brief bright glow
of the fireflies' dance along the track.

That first breath
broken to ripple on a railway
promised permanent movement,
fanned that leap from the Steppes to Paris
chinked that iron cracked by grey-suited men
and womanlight of candles bright
against prayer walls

and curtains ...
rich, red, velveteen blue
opening to frame Nureyev, Fonteyn
opening to frame a flicker,
a soupçon etched in perfect arabesque.

You could never have lived to be a hundred
for you only came to dance.
Floorboards were only springboards

that dance on the plains of a migrant's pain
flickered through cities to rekindle an awe
grown dull
in our restless, corporate souls.

I'll never see Nureyev dance now
but fireflies flickering along that track
ignite a luminescent spark
fire some soft, low, wild rhythm
my words are feebly trying
to follow.

Fireflies

The instances of immigrants
are drawn from half-remembered breaths
where sepia is fringed by new tomorrows,

passages dismembered, dance out into this light
where mirrored incandescences
beat graceful soundless wings;
are fireflies beneath a skin
that flutters, paperthin

here subterranean halls
are stacked like breakers yards:
paper bags and grips
new suits, our clan smell

here lie those who chose
walked, not ran
planned, paid, prepared
rinsed rich watercolours with the flatness of palms
potter's arms stretched to tease straight lines
from abstractions of vision

beyond this be dragons:
villages with beaches,
unpolluted springs
ricefields, coco-
palms:

wet, smooth, cemented
we are crafter and crafted
we are clay
flour balls, dough
rolled, curled like conchshells
fantailed for translation

here - my lover says - a mango from your country
its forceripe too-sweet juices
dribbles on its journey
re-enters those dark passages
those kitchens made of wood
those textured subterranean halls
where fireflies light the darkness
those villages of words
where photographs scalloped by woodant bites
die natural deaths, instead of languishing,
martyrs in sepia

in the dark of my wardrobe
my tapestried stilletoes beam
a special phosphorescence
their mirrored incandescences and paper fireflies
seek brass, wood, water
where my photographs and favourite witch resides

here - he slices neatly with a knife
and slides a trembling segment down my sacrificial throat

SPIRIT/LANDS

Confessions of the Unoriginal

Adulteress, then.

Then
they flung stones
missiled by anger
slicing into skin still warm
from their fingers
and the dry-clay dust

Then
cries were stifled
sandals ran, filtered palm leaf
shadows on stone

The Pride of the Mother turning to shame
Marys, Magdalenes
remembered, revered
two from the many
seed and stain, running red,
run red into grain

I plead innocence, Massa, sir
Innocence, Massa, sir

ooooooooooooooooooooooooooooooooooooooooooooooooooooooooo

Adulteress, now.

Back-back out of shadow of steeple and bell
seeking the confessor
Me, the somnambulist,
Me, limbo walker
Me, bimbo, Woman

Limbolands

I walk streets
post-biblically earned
where right and wrong merge
bend to the angle of the sun
here screaming is coded but colourful
the devil a victim of childhood

but
hells receding with virgin births
still leave their ashes behind
moist Ash Wednesdays -
where seedling confessors
spring up, break earth
line paths like mirrors
offer crystals
reclassify venials, mortal

without a hell we grant ourselves permission

ooooooooooooooooooooooooooooooooooooooooooooooooooooooo

in this, my creature I walk
my feet curl on stone
flatten on dirt
liquidise in water

I travel my reasons my seasons my seeds
I travel my corncircles
I travel my thoughts my words my deeds
crucified rosary beads

Full and big bellied they travel me
from soul to womb to soul
from soul to womb to soul

ooooooooooooooooooooooooooooooooooooooooooooooooooooooo

I plead innocence massa, sir
in the name of evolution
in the name of preservation
in the quest for more and more
for less will never do

it never did when stones came flying
missiled by anger
slicing into skin
still warm from their fingers and the dust

ooooooooooooooooooooooooooooooooooooooooooooooooo

begging your pardon sir
I met a fallen angel sir   (just like me)
crammed with desire sir
stuffed with illusion sir   (just like me)
we found all the candles sir
lit them end to end
his laughter cut like headlamps
lace-embroidering the ceiling
I suppose he's just a shit - Just like me.

and through the stained glass door
where our junk mail falls
diamond-patterned shadows still
slant through the grills
the cold of the confessional still
chills to the bone
priest-tones soft still
dry cough dribble
like pebbles on stone
reaching to grant me absolution

penance blow hot
penance blow cold
penance wash me clean
at nine days old

I'll take my penance massa, sir
here, find yourself a stone
missiled by anger, fuelled by my sin
it will slice the skin of woman
through womb into bone.

Litanies

Where litanies layered the lacquered floor
there too lay you
where Basilica blues tinged Her robe
there worshipped you
where stone bowls cupped the Lourdes
there too flowed you
your fingers vaulted like Cathedral ceilings
interior concave spines
rippling prayers
travelling in whispers
through sacred inner spaces
and i say and say
Mother of ...
pray for us
Mother of ...
pray for us
Mother of ...
pray for us

Glorias

Christmas Eve
the town is out
streets as bright as day
wild lights ripple the eaves of Government House
reflect the raucous laughing of Ladies of the Night
teetering along Water Street
diamanté necklaces glittering like tinsel
echoing the lights of ships in dock
garlands on merchandise, matelots released

Families well-frocked
fingers interlocked
windowshop Main Street
en-route for the Cathedral

Ready for the chorus of Glorias
in Excelsis, in Creole
Ave Marias in English
Kyries in Latin

Tinsel
street lights
Glorias in high heels
running
laughing
sing in tongues.

The Devil Child

Sassy, Mamma seh, Sassy!
Eyepass, Cookie seh, eyepass
And mek the sign o the cross with spit
Across she forehead

Spirit! Uncle Bo seh, Spirit!
She gon take the boys for a ride
And with a sprinkle o rum from he glass
He christen the devil child

The child run, beat drum
With she finger pon the pew
Fidget with pantie elastic
Tap foot on altar floor before communion

Lawd Lawd! Them seh
Lawd Lawd.

Doors

convent door slamming, hollow
through the years
wakening shadows on migrant faces
shadows that once fell on grassland
flattened by Dutchmen, running Blackmen
racing souls that melt like water
on hot dusty roads

child watches Mummy running
racing thru corridors

19

to the sound of the giro falling
from the letterbox to the floor
what does she care about Dutchmen
or women that they stole
from shackled Ashanti Blackmen
who fell crying through convent doors?

Lilies of the Field

years later, when the scent came
it was always lily-shaped
incarnating through wardrobe doors
the dining room window

during the wake when the cocktail of rum
and prayers had threatened to display the bier
it was lily-of-the-valley they sprinkled on ice
and lilies of the field we became

Them Ah Call

Them ah call, them ah call
Them ah call from the shadows
and i turn my head to the shadows
but there's no-one there
but shadows

Here! We are here!
i hear them whisper
and i slip my step to the rhythm
but i dance with shadows
there's no-one here
but shadows

See! We are here
here! H E R E!
And their sounds bounce off
of an ancient drum
and my fingers slip
on the grip of my thumb
on my suitcase

I laugh
I cry
I'm looking
But there's only shadows
only shadows.

FATHER/LANDS

the limbo walkers

i siddown wit mih fadda by dih rivuh
he dead dead   we know dat
dih berbice waters wetting he feet not mine

ah point mih finguh cross dih oddah side
traveller dem lining up an waiting
dih water she licking dem toe slow slow

some brave already
dem eye ah fall out see dey cyan walk pon dih water
dey lif dey head up high like sugarcane
dem spirit rise up high   hise straight up to dih sky

i turn wateh mih daddy
he say is the limbo walkers dem

these then are the limbo walkers!
(limbo did mean a different ting one time ...)
dey grips pile up high pon dih riverside
dey mouth flappin like fish in dih air
dey eyes runnin on dih water
waitin dere turn to walk her

i sit wit mih daddy by dih rivuh
he dead we both know dat
i visit him in dreams
in dese he sharin miracles wit me
miracles dat in life he dint have time to free
dat time he captain ships and chauffeur barges through
Kwakwani shores
he long trips away from home
makin fun fuh we twistin momma finguh easy easy

we dint have no time to talk
we chilren mouth them
flap like fish
we fraid o' daddy
daddy walk long
tall in he job
an big like captain

is only now we makin time
to watch the Berbice runnin fas
to watch she eddies spiral splints o' bark an mangrove
leaves
an floatin ferry boat an people dem wit ease
is only now we makin time
to name she colours
red for bauxite, gold an blood
blue an yellow boat oil spinnin
runnin out from underneath dih stellin

we dint have no time to talk
we chilren mouth dem
flap like fish
we fraid o' daddy
daddy walk long
tall in he job
big like captain

all dis wilderness, only dih rivuh lef wile
dey cyant tame she
train she or chain she
sometime a image cross mih mind
she's a girl chile runnin
naked wicked an wile

we dint have no time to talk
we chilren mouth dem flap like fish
we fraid o' daddy
daddy long gone
tall in he job an big
like captain

dih same way how she carry he
pon dem bauxite trips
dat he captain ships
up to dat Kwakwani
dih same way she hisin me
wit mih bag an grip
chain belt swingin from mih hip
board dih ferry Torani

　　we dint have no time to talk
　　we chilren mouth dem flap like fish
　　we fraid o' daddy daddy walk long
　　tall in he job an big like captain

when he dead dey say go girl
hise yuh tail outa dis place
dere int no room fuh no mixrace
whiteface goldhair girl
find yuh education
lef dih Berbice to she own pace
wash mih footprint lef no trace
i gone to another worl

　　we dint have no time to talk we chilren
　　mouth it flap like fish we fraid
　　o' daddy daddy walk long tall
　　in he job an big like captain

an is limbo mih limbo misself
an mih walk like crab on land
an when dey ask where do you come from
mih mouth it flap like fish is choke i choke
an dey gimmih glassa water.

For All The Seeds Planted by Men in Foreign Soils and Left to Harvest Themselves

Lawd Jesus bring mih Daddy back
Ma say he gone ah Englun
I promise i an gon fight no more
Mek he come back from tha Englun

I siddown here in the bottom house
So Ma won't catch me crying
She send 'Natius for a quart o' rum
Soon she temper will be flying

I an mind if i get the cane
For walking lika big woman
I gon watch mih mouth, na answer back
Just you come back from tha Englun

Hush hush lick lick mih gon shut mih mouth
I gon mind mih business
I promise i gon work hard at school
And help Ma in the house

Lawd Jesus since mih Daddy gone
It seem that Ma don't want we
She lash out with the wild cane
If we so much as watch she

She say she can't stand blue eye
Is like he lef his ghost behind
She say how we is her cross to bear
And no-one else will want she

No-one want white man leftovers
No-one want us white man pickney
No-one want Ignatius and me
They call we whitey-shitey

Lawd Jesus bring mih Daddy back
At least sos he could tell we
Why he leave us Ma and we
And walk and gone ah Englun

In the Wake of the Santa Maria

We read of the Santa, the Pinta, the Nina
in the cool of a timbered school room
under threat of the cane we pattered
Amo, Amas, Amant

Like others we left the sweet smell of cane
black rain across a blue window
wild cane across our young backs
in the name of education

Nobody wanted to hear, Las Casas
Nobody wanted to hear

Like others I wake in the night silentscreaming
quiet, so the children won't hear

like others woken ancestors ago
to the sound of the thief in the night

manacled, tossed into a bellyblack hold
over newly charted seas
half a life climbing coconut trees
white shirts like sails fanning palm leaves
scanning the skies for the Indies

Truth, like woman, is adaptable.

The price of Shakespeare on brown lawns, seesaws,
was to fall, ripe fruit on the wayside
spending hours of life in a dream.

Woman, nurturer, carer, floating
swell of surreal wave
one arm for a child and one for a dream
washing up in a close embrace

Dreamstates paint pollution blue
where manacles rust below
past oil-slicked Santa Marias
and bright, brochured Bequias

I ignored the cries of my mothers
on my dreamstate return

Are you too at my shoulders, Las Casas?
My father is turning his back

In the black of the hold did you know could you see
that one day I would stare out of multicoloured eyes
and try to write about you?

Maggie Harris

I Am the Mythmaker, Said He

Arachne and Anancy meet to throw the dice again
she with a wisp of silver greying at the temple
he with a lilt of that selfsame skip
and the curve of an ivory cane

Immortality had lost its appeal in countless battles of wit
in duels and shiftings and endless fencings
constant redefinings
of mortality and myth

Their masters had long retired
their transformations straddling theories and sexes
dwelling now on that mystic realm
where faith alone shoulders confrontation

Representatives had been and gone
some staying far too long, some almost daring
bearing gifts of children
offering use of the Third Eye, a New Age
a Fourth and Fifth, Aquarian Dimension

But Arachne and Anancy both had stayed
the trickster and the weaver both replayed
through parallels of conciousness, the rolling of the dice
the setting of the pattern, tapestries displayed ...

Which tale?
Rapunzel!

Limbolands

Up in the tower
Rapunzel's weaving
Samson's power

At the battlements
neat tree-lined avenues
converge

from the up-hill down-dale
pleasantness
where high taxation

benefits
in flexi-time and childcare by the hour.

Rapunzel lays down
her silver mirror
crossing her pretty brow, a frown

The prince is late
again; steering the Mercedes
out of town

tests his leadership
to the full, against
his people's needs

and world needs, should he
send the refugees home
or simply

run them down?

Alexander had ways, Arachne yawned
Darius had means, so what's changed?
I'll spin you the tale of Curtis my friend
to while away the day.

On a northern shore
feet stamp from the cold
no amount of years

can erase
the longing for the sun
where once

El Dorado had called
from the north now
the pier points south

Curtis's fingers clutch
fur collar upturned
with knuckles the colour of bone.

Home.

Slim shade, sugarcane parasol
only white men risked
that twelve o'clock sun

but those that yearned
ran barefeet
heading for the creek

(I suspect your prince was one of these)

seeking a brief utopia
running from the master role
and wild, implausible morals.

Limbolands

(Wild? Did we ever run wild or did we like your
dressmaker's child
need to fashion a soul out of memories
that unravel forever like time?)

Foot-bottom skin hard
on new, raw earth
Curtis's feet, the colour of dirt

had never run on tennis courts
or plunged in estate pools
his dressmaker mother fetched him

time and again
heading for the bush
going home.

On the backdam the dressmaker's house
throbbed day in
throbbed day out

whirred with the sound of the Singer machine
image seekers climbing frontsteps
changing sneakers for stilettoes

clutching magazine pictures
of Doris Days, Ava Gardners,
bearing lengths of peau-de-soie

lace, and crepe de chine.
Curtis sitting on the front porch
traded sweets for rubber bands

trapping the souls of chicken hawks
wild, wired kitepaper blue
framed triangled red.

Anancy skipped and threw the dice
blowing on his palms
let's have the prince remembering
his life before this ice:

> Massa Prince climbed wearily
> up his lady's hair
> seeking the comfort of the breast

> a rest from stock control
> and mining
> and lost geographies.

> In the dreamtime small
> feet run from the creek
> where Anancy, sit

> ting on a lily
> leaf laughed with a clap
> of the hands and fash

> ioned a sail out of
> sugarcane leaves. There
> Rapunzel stroked the roots

> of his miniscule plantation
> and briskly called his name

> until he came.

> Kiskadees called
> through treetops heavy
> with rain, singing

black crows huddled on wires
telegraph poles looped
like Liberty swags

at battlement doors. There
Rapunzel wrapped baby up
tucked baby up

into the crevice
of her care.

Her lullaby rockabyed
lullabyed down
lulling and dulling in turn

dispersing anaesthesia
out into the streets
of town.

It's the dreams! Anancy cackled
holding his belly in as it rolled
and black brocade and silver rippled
the prince tossed in his tower
pygmies drummed, headhunters danced
and Rapunzel lay naked sucking tubes of sugarcane.

You are a fool, Anancy, Arachne slowly drawled
the time has passed for blame to be laid
always at women's door. And anyroad all that's now
has gone before, all that's to be has been,
that's one thing you and I
ought to know for sure.

Anancy leant on his ivory cane
a gleam in one rheumy eye
I tell you time and time again,
it's not if you get there but how!

> I am the mythmaker I
> perpetuating vision
> wining and dining and players all
> - pieces you and I

Dawn broke before the players spoke
both crystallized the morning
sweat that clung to hair draped dew
across the breast across the chest of Rapunzel and Prince.

With one long nail he traced her cheek
still smudged with print from evening play
while A & A still scissored lay
in mimicry and majesty and ink

MOTHERLANDS

" ... in my mother's house there are many
mansions ..."

Mansions?

Her eyebrows lift to sculpt that perfect arch
of cathedral windows   doors through which her mantillad
head
had ever bowed, the tap of sandalled, cubaned, stilettoed
heels
beating on stone and greenheart floors.

Passage to this house is always accessible   as lambs we beat
bleating paths to her door
that faith, solid as St. Peter's rock
counsels, intersects words like   trust, hope.

Her skirt was ample enough to hide beneath
its fifties flare defined by its time
covered thighs that leant against sinks
bent besides mangles, spread to birth us.

Later they buckled under the weight of blind old women
staggered with dishes up long hospital stairs
bowed in English pews, sinews taut against the cold

In my mother's house there are many mansions
many rooms empty of sound rich in image:
petals in a brass bowl, a candlelit altar
a row of china dolls on her bed ...her dancing with a glass
of Banks beer miming to Frankie Avalon ...

The lacquered floors, creamed with Mansion Polish
mirrored the red of the Sacred Heart, the blue of His eye.

Her passage through rooms jangled like wind chimes,
rosary beads, gold bangles ...
we could always hear her coming

In my mother's house there are many mansions ...

Her path to our doors now is always well laden
a dish of cook-up rice, a packet of tea
a jar of cassareep, a pumpkin ...
her Guyanese ways have remoulded their shape
fanned their feathers to fit
like the Corentyne house of her childhood whose
mansions

breathed away its walls
welcomed both virgin and spirit
incanted new sacred spaces
where our feet now pace.

These now are the rooms we enter
like Alice we fall, we sink, we grow
in my mother's house the card walls fall
floors shift to doors, pause on shores.

In my mother's house there are many mansions

there by the grace of God, forever wander I.

Warrior

You passed me the sword and wept
knowing how your own mother had passed you sheaves of
corn
and you had had to borrow scythes to slice the
undergrowth.

The scars were on your feet still
from battering paths clear through fields of stubbled cane,
so you lined mine with banana leaves and reeds

pulled from the riverside,
bound them with that mud whose gullies bore the trace of
so many warriors:
the Yoruba, the Akan, the Ashanti.

You sprinkled me with water made holy by the priest
but in your back room charged the spirits with my safety
invoked Yemanja and Kali, and sacrificed Demetrius, your
cockerel,
with one quick, sharp slice of the throat.

Recorded into the praise-songs of my leaving
was the news that I left not as a bride,
my charging from the tribe was that of warrior-scout

and many more would follow.
(Some on the arms of borrowed men
who promised them a northern El Dorado)

How were you to know that times would change
beyond all comprehension?
That the time for swords, too, would pass
would fly by in one short generation and again we need

the time for words, for praise-songs to the elders
memories to weave within the skins of our children.

Last night I dreamt of you: you had crossed the water
just like Yemanja did -
but this time,
what you passed me was my pen.

Chrysalis

For months she inhabited darkened spaces,
corners where walls leant and light declined to enter.
The presence of shadows followed her footsteps
glided along the stairs, paused in that wide space
between the nursery door where paper butterflies danced
above the cot.

Between us too, walls
too solid to penetrate, a womb-like world
dis-similar twins swum
wearing our loss like armour
clumsy like tortoises in a carpeted seascape.

With the coming of summer, intruders arrived:
moths, bumblebees, earwigs
flying through open windows
curling through loose brick
battening our faces with diaphanous wings.

I reached for weapons; shoes, rolled newspapers ...
her anger rose like a dustsheet
smothering me with its dense air,
her thin arms flailing like reeds.

She carried the moth into the garden
releasing it through cupped palms
that rose to cover her face.

I watched but kept my distance.
Over the weeks her rounded shoulders
wandered the garden, dismantled the cot
made a cold frame;

gathered seed heads from dead wallflowers, dying
cornflowers
sweet peas browning on the fence.

This morning I followed her sharp cry
breaking from the roses in the sun;
for the first time in nine long months
she smiled
and lifted her small hand to my mouth.

Swallowing Seawater

Small boys, their penises curled
like whelks against doe skin
run

I watch them idly
scanning the dark sweep of sand
where my daughter tests a midnight sea

Like the turning tide
her limbs are lit now and then
by the scalloped lips
of a grudging, cloud-bound moon

She has just learnt to swim.

I have compressed my own lips
pinioned my limbs to the sand
the salt on the air has me
swallowing seawater
endlessly.

Voices rise out of the darkness
young, crisp, with the dry cackle of crones;

"Watchyer! Show us yer headlamps!
Go on! Letshavealook!"

Venus-like
her bronze skin
milks out of shadows
her seaweed hair cropped close around that face
that bears the barest wisp of a smile

I curl my cellular thighs
deeper into the tartan rug.
My fist uncurls.
My throat is dry.

Fifteen

Fifteen
I remember Fifteen
weighed down with soul
feeling
carrying
mouthfuls of pain
running
holding
breath in
up the stairs

Fifteen
In the picture
that I carry
you are three
gold curls   Fifteen
tumbling   I remember Fifteen
sweet   bicycle burning streets
baby blue eye face   wriggling hot

your infant
English accent
rolling Ds
around Dub
and Cs
around Calypso
trading my memory
dancing Marley Reggae
under pretend banana trees

and Catholic
cool Trade Winds
wet kisses
hungry boys
   coming from or going
overseas

      Fifteen swayed
      high, low
        snailed
        pubescent beauty
        matchstick legs
      on N/A* streets
      priests, nuns, Americans
      temples, weddings,
        festivals, cane
      Bingo, Bridge, English women

fairy light bright Convent grounds
minutes walk away
from rocksteady dancehalls
rumshops
where loud women
sold their love away

Fifteen
your Fifteen
computers, Adidas
discman sounds
hugged the schoolyard walls
and
long
fingers
of substances
beckoned

* *New Amsterdam*

44

from
shadows

Your Fifteen learnt of partings
the breaking down of doors   and divorce
long Sunday afternoons waiting   like death
broken promises   hurts
and hate spinning out of mouths   like Fifteen once
only meant   weighed
                       down
for kisses   with soul
                      feeling
               mouthfuls of pain
                running
                holding
              breaths in
              up the stairs

My
Fifteen
followed
a coffin, sought
shelter under tress
Fifteen seeking shelter under real banana trees.

Fifteen
jumping up from nowhere
hit me in the face
your coltlike beauty
disguising inner grace
You cut
bits of paper
draw, fold   battling origami wars
colour, paste   with baby sisters
breathless   and I pray

Maggie Harris

running   how I pray,
poetry   you won't lay down your violin
trillion word essays   for a Sainsbury's concerto
                                on a rush of trolley wheels

At fourteen, my baby still
but how do I know
how can I say
what you smelt
what you thought
what you touched
in those long long schooldays
in that wakening between perception's guise
and momma's baby's eyes
in that space between
what you think
and what you say
to me?

You hated boys, thank God!
you may escape
the waiting
that sweep of your face
to the window
your ear to the sound
of the gate
that dry teenage cough
in the street
the hope,
in a bicycle bell

no re-readings of Barret-Browning
no relish of Tennyson's Maud
no sharp swift jump
from Nancy Drew to the Count of Mills and Boon

46

Fifteen

a curtain falls over your eyes
there is
no giggling
no tumbling
no wild somersaulting
no pasting
no sticking
no singing in tune
no more violin
only No and Not and Nothing
you are In Love

and I, the mother dragon
and breathing fire from the hill
and mother dragons never understand

But! there's so much
 so much
  I want to say!
  To tell you
  of love
   tell you to beware
   what sets the feet
   a-dancing
   and the heart
   hung crying
   from a string
  to tell you ...
  of love
   and early morning waking
   head hanging out the window
  ear listening for that sound
 of the dry teenage cough in the street
 and the hope, in a bicycle bell!

Maggie Harris

I want to tell you of love
as you flick through magazines
where the Facts of Life scream out

in bold black lettering
in cold red lettering
ABORTION! AIDS! SEX! All you need to know!

But my stained Catholic heart recoils
and part of me is pleased
these things are being done for me
they're sparing me the need

        Fifteen still residing
        like a kernel deep inside
        dries my tongue
        (O Jezebel)
        Fifteen still residing
        like a kernel deep inside
        remembering asking
        of the parenting of Eve
        of parenting ...

        So what can I tell you
        that you don't already know
        what can I tell you
        that I think you need to know?

        You will walk your own road
        but I know Fifteen
        and dragons
        and they can understand.

For Aimee

my baby came running down the street
crying from the thunder
pressing her small face
into the white of my skirt

the dirt from the park
streaked across her face
like the staggered zigzag paths
of tyre tracks

and i say, shush my baby shush
it's only the rain fighting the sun
shush, my baby shush
it's only clouds in boxing gloves
punching their way out of town

my baby hung onto my arm, trembling
running for home
that safe box of bricks and mortar
built to keep the fear out
and the care in

and i can say shush as she turns in my skirt
shush as i shut the door
smile as i wipe her eyes
all the time knowing

there are other babies running
running from guns, running
running from bombs, running
running from sometime love, running
down roads and avenues

away from what they call home
that safe box of bricks and mortar
built to keep the fear out
and the care in.

Blame

of course i am to blame
how can one raise goddesses if we can't spell their names
of course i am to blame
i made so many promises describing rain
real rain, ejected from a sky
twice as large three times as hard
as these piffling raindrops here
which trickle and then disappear

of course i am to blame
how can one chant praise-songs to fields and plains
your children never claimed
of course i am to blame
i told so many stories, nancy lies
anansi tricking crocodiles
mongoose and mancrow
brother crab and others they don't know

of course i am to blame
i am ashamed, i bow my head in shame
i didn't know Kanaima's name
Yemanja never came, but then again
i did not come prepared, was ill-advised
self-willed, a child
promised to a mothering
not stranded, exiled on these shores

so if my children dance to other drums
and speak in different tongues
whose fault is it but mine?
of course i am to blame
i never knew Kanaima's name
Yemanja never came
of course i am to blame.

Sextet

1: *The Changeling*

- slithered out noiselessly
fist cuffed, but not surprisingly
as babies go.

Whimsical, with a smile
that stirred puddles
she practised her winsomeness
on dock leaves, bottled milk
her father's wellies with shards of glass.

She shapeshifted easily
as troglets do
the soft chimpanzee hair
- at first appearance like soft down
on the forested velveteen body -

grew spikes overnight
re-inforced the gnoming
in a weathering of storms
that fidgeted restlessly at windowpanes
whose lightning slashed staggered replies
to her yodelling.

At first we were amused, detached,
she was a cyber pet adept at stamping ...

that was before suspicion dawned
that her rhythms were not quite as ordered as our own
But anyroad,
we loved our changeling
she was ou' own.

2: *Rocking the Cradle*

... the incredible thing is
her beauty still haunts, has the power to haunt
despite all.

... teases the mind back to cradles, first steps
the uncurl of fat fingers on Dumpton Gap sands ...

The mind is dysfunctional
replays Andalucia, seduced by that arm
and its cigarette curl, misreading

the lip, those blackberry lips
the 'fuck-yous' like fall-out
the wars about lipstick
skirts up her bum
the raw sea-side accent
that salts off the sides of Ford Escorts

It still sees Spanish shoes, oak floors and mirrors
reflecting the promise of futures where mothers
are doing their duty of planting and rooting
not
squaring small shoulders like warriors.

Sorry Dorothy,* but
the hand that rocks the cradle
no longer rules the world.

3: 13, With a Fist

... in the trail of the knife the scar sleeps   neat   white
bleached like buffalo ribs across the plain.
my fingers limp, track its crimpled edges
where once flew flags of feathers, red for birth.

... they flew ragged as

your howling started fires
blew smoke rings
and you danced in
on watermelon trains

... scarlet feathers

waving as you danced
in your own wild rhythm
that xeroxed over landscapes
tornadoed dustbowls

... twisters
orchestrating that howling
baying at suns, moons, ridges
the boundaries of plains
where your shadow danced before you

they called your birth 'a section'/now your spirit is a knife
sharp steel twisting diamonds/trellises of blue/ sky-shaped
patterned ribs of bone/it shreds red feathers into ribbons of

* *Dorothy Dinnerstein- 'The hand that rocks the cradle rules the world'*

Maggie Harris

sand/cuts into the whites of scars/lifts and forms into the
shape of a fist/small hands that curled around my finger so/
just thirteen moons ago.

 4: *By any other name* ...

Is that you mi ama?
(a hibiscus by any other name ...)

Is that you running out into this cobbled street
whose curtains mark
your fourteen year old legs hurling
into a throbbing nissan sunny?

aah cara, i thought i had loved you well
cradling and crooning
i thought it had been enough
teasing your hair through my fingers
singing you songs about brown skin girls
and the wild wide demerara

aah but maybe those tales were wrong for now
wrong for this time
our mermaids were women not disneys
our pocahontas skinned labas too
but what do you know of these?
and where, how could they breathe here
on grey stone?

so this is you carita/chakari
arm on the hip
rocking on platform soles
your bubblegum a question mark between us ...

5: *The Meeting*

"A little background if you could
- just to help us get a picture
see if we can understand
where Carita's coming from.

You've been divorced I see
and Mum has custody?
But Dad does have access...
Yes I see.

Of course these situations are difficult
but believe me, I've seen worse
if it helps you feel any better,
you're not the only ones!

So when did truancy start?
The school has voiced concern ...
and you were not aware?
Parents do their best, it's only fair!

I see Carita used to dance!
I'm quite surprised.
Oh please don't take offence!
The term 'deprived' is not at all implied.

Well I think we've come quite far today
Don't worry about Carita's reticence
At least she's here!
Well shall we say six weeks hence, say 18th Feb? That's
great!"

6: *Lake Christmas*

That Christmas, we took to the fells
anointed ourselves in its waters
understood the blessing
was to be there at all.

As travellers, we were one short
but knew that her absence
had initiated our presence there
had sent us reeling

four hundred motorway miles
through blizzards
seeking a solace only to be found
amongst great depths and heights.

The owner of the cottage
loaned us a plastic Christmas tree
which leaned absurdly against a windowpane
struggling against its own inability to frame

Derwentwater, substituted chintz.
On Boxing Day it rained. We watched
the brave backpack their children
up Cat Bells in bright yellow waterproofs

that took me back to Berbice
where snorkelled yellow-clad councilmen
sprayed mosquito larvae in the grass
around our school.

(Those Christmases are with me still
lingering their absences in memories
of waters dark with histories
which this adopted land cannot replace.)

But we made the best of things
worked at our delight
at being there; stopping the car
above Bassentwaite to contemplate

that still, yet undulating place
whose beauty leaves a residue
that scratches at the arteries
and mixes joy and pain like metaphors, in frames.

Now these years on I struggle still
to redefine that Christmas,
that urge to celebrate a birth
whilst drowning both in beauty and amniotic symmetry.

I couldn't answer then as you
wine glass in hand asked, happy?
But floating up from Christmas wrappings
pressed my face flat up against the pane.

Hurricane

So:
There should be a quartet of black horses
All with plumes, all thoroughbreds, biting at the bit
Their wild energy harnessed in a shine of silver buckles
Yet with restraint in that toss of the head, that tilt
That will make this the most English of processions.

In the quiet of country lanes I see you
Or the wide sweep of a city street on Sundays past
Either would do. I can see your stunning beauty true
To form: sleek black hair, Rose Red on a Surbiton bypass
Riding Snow W's borrowed glass bier - all for attention.

Somewhere there will be an orange grove, there I will lay
you to rest
With all the ritual that memory can unglove.
I will draw those women out of the trees to wail and beat
their breasts
With the sun piercing the lace of their mantillas.

Of course they will gather me too, shawled
Into the comfort of that closing, into that soft entombing
That smells of lavender presses and bottles of Limacol
Sugarwater and fresh pods of cotton
And the high sweet fruit-scent of fallen sapodillas.

I shall bury you in a strong wind
With a bite in each gust, evoke Hurricane Anne
From those bastards The Trades, endlessly circling
A tired Atlantic, migrants in all but name.
She'll whip up something rotten eh?

Force expletives into this eloquence
We grandly called our own, with bursts of Coleridge
Peppering out of our backyards presuming an eloquence
So quickly ditched,
So swiftly discarded by your "fuck you mother".

> There was one such as you I recall
> I can't remember her name, or her face
> Only that we were warned to walk, swift pass her door
> And never play, nor encourage her to call.
> I lie. I do recall her smile - it lit her wholeness
> Like a moon and paid her early passage to Curaçao
> Whilst we remained in school chanting Chillon
> And someone who was
> " walking with great beauty into the night".

Yes, I'll evoke Anne.
She'll whip the Demerara up from her endless rinsing of
relics.
She'll come, ushering bridesmaids of small green crabs
So swiftly to their exodus
They'll never know their passage 'till its made.

Anger often guests at gravesides
Etched between the latticework of tears
Edged in each prod and thrust of the spade's slice.
It tenses beneath those pellets of stones which spray
The earth, courses the earth like a virus

Paws at the pocked earth with shoes burnished
To a fine sheen. And another false creed we had presumed,
That such passion that furnished
Those sacred pages spilt over into the cobbled streets
Was present in each grasp of the hand, each negotiated
trust.

Rippled with the same surged blood, the same passage
That we had coursed beneath the self-same sun.

Shall there be attendants? Yes of course!
And black armbands. And cavalcades accompanying the
hearse
Where silent men will raise their hats
And women draw the veil.

Admit it, who has not laughed once at those backwaters
Where ladies still wore gloves, still moved like manatees
Still brewed the tea at cricket matches?
But they mourned for longer then, even in their whirling
within worlds
Even though uneasy at those funerals where women

Flung themselves screaming into open graves
Raking at the coffins which imprisoned their beloveds.

But I had been released from such a past,
Such tasks of savagery have no place in these small green
fields,
As have neither crabs, nor manatees.
So it may be 'in the blood' as they say, a residue of Jezebel
residing
Surfacing to rake her nails across your face for daring to
disobey
The Mother.

Thus they came armed to legislate, silent and polite
Dignified, unlike us who wailed loud into the night,
remembering stonings
Remembering slices of hearts still beating on sacrificial
stones.

Hurricane!

Even the syllables play at puns
Hurri
-cane.

Which came first? The storm, the crop, the planters
Whom in naming, conquered, christened, stamped
Their graven images
(In the beginning was the word ...)
So swiftly, that immediacy itself became an act of re/
possession?

Images are what remain:
The dark ash of a burnt field clouding the town
A child with a book by a darkened window
A black servant sweeping the yard with a broom.

The glint of a cutlass edge in the moonlight
Rustling young shoots in the cane
That ripple that slits the skin like a slate
And moved one poet to claim
"The hurricane does not roar in pentameter!"*

Only now I realise your helplessness
You, sucked up like rooftops and whole villages
Swept along in the wake of those peers equally
Though differently, as versed as I
You with a blood rushing that gush faster and only me as a
dam
To hold you
Fine dam, alone on this crazy river which I still can't spell
Fine dam.

But let me end as I began
Exorcise you as fittingly as befits your passion
We both know this grieving will never come to an end
Nevertheless I shall bury it accordingly,
One final epitaph:

May the builders of dams
Constantly keep an eye to the sky;
Watch for the God, Hurican.

I Refuse To Call You Mother

the landing was easy, one straight flight
ignorant of Icarus
home to the mother country
airport yards busy with the diesel throb of progress
smooth concrete, bright lights,
motorways ribboning, no anacondas,
no red dust slicing through rainforest

* *Quote from Brathwaite,* History of the Voice

believing the initiation rite to be language
i soon fell, a stranger to the smell of things
recognising no Prospero, no Narcissus

i cried then for my own land where swifts and condors soar
for the angry red of rivers, corials on the shore
calypsos and name places, like Kaieteur
and in this wild lamentation i beat fist to breast
and felt a fool

but -
you sent great winds before me which i was slow to see
Saharan sands and hurricanes that raked you in their
wanderings
pinned me to your fallen oaks
to listen to your wooded heart beneath its tarmaced tomb.
they were migrants too, and i an Ariel released
traced you like a lover, stroked moss and belly-bark
and Pan, gauche and dark
in chalk and downland grasses.

and you - a tad coquettish in your trick of seasons
wearing at your will autumn's copper or summer's maniacal
fetish
led me to the slaughter, vixen-trapped in brash bright
headlights
copper-toned and brush-red moon-honed road.

but even though your parallels seduce
i refuse to call you Mother
knowing the misuse imbued in such a name.
instead i say canoe, not corial
kingfisher for hummingbird
learn those fisherwoman's ballads of the sea
released, my sapling tongues emerge

and hymn and rap
and swing and shout:
herein my native land
herein
my
native
l/
and.

Emerald, Just One Colombian Mountain

i said i'd never call you mother
and yet, and yet,
is that not your belly ripped
by fingernails and spades
mechanical diggers, land-rover wheels
bare feet and Parisian shoes?

like rats my fellow humans scramble
this hollowed out chasm
with gold-tipped fountain pens, weighing scales
sieving the ashes of your feet
with eyes glazed green and riveted

your roots dangle like lank hair
loose in crumbling earth
a thin aureole of emerald foliage
crowning the broken ridge of the skyline
like a balding man with his back to the sun.

Maggie Harris

Burrowing Through Bellies

and through my mother's belly burrowed
long-tailed spermatozoa
fertile
sturdy little chaps
wearing tin helmets

a protection,
against her contractile spasms
her chasms,
fissures of an acrid nature.

confined,
the mushroom computer-read its D.N.A.
scanned its capacity for change
it abandoned its tin helmet
sought its exit
through strata on strata
plate on plate
where sleeping volcanic gases
stirred and yawned
into coils of snaking fallopian tubes.

its explosion was a silent matter
it couldn't compete with football kings
or winners of lottery jackpots

only the smallest of borders carried his name,
they called him Nuke.

Onwards

the hands of women are like water running
dipping calabash full
calabash ladle Guyana water
running sandbank red

woman-sway of sexuality soothed
like billycan water
carried up from the river into the cry
of a sakiwinki
into the call
of a kiskadeee
the tickle of the tide erasing
every footprint
in the sand

the hands
of slave women
rinsed repentance
into the scars
cleansing, easing
seeming to forgive
the power of a silent tongue growing
from generations
o n w a r d s

through green walls tall
the rivers
passed time
from an unseen mouth
through lengths
through breadths

of crabwood
greenheart
mora trees
riverbends lost
in their twists and turns
their
l a z y
s n a k i n g

o n w a r d s

the faces of women
rose like water
under the thatch
of red mud houses
their palms rose up
serrated fingers
panelling their anguish
stifling their waiting cries
for husbands who were porknockers
for husband who sailed ships
for husbands who escaped the whip
to learn to wield the whip

and whilst the river grew silent-tongued
and swollen with their power
they formed themselves into tributaries
unlocked the voices their mothers had stored
and continued the journey

o n w a r d s.

Migrant Woman Bodysong

This is the shape of my country she said
and she trailed my finger from the sky of
her brow to her throat where the pulse beat
    its heartime. This is the shape of my
      country she said and we climbed the
        ridges of the Pakoraima Mountains
          whose chill made peaks
        of her nipples. This is the shape
      of my country she said and we wandered
    the plains where the Rupununi savannahed her
belly. This is the shape of my country she said
and dipped her fingers in rivers where otter
smells dampened and lingered.   This is the
shape of my cunt
ry   she said
and   i   lost   my   way
          and ilostmyway
            in her forest.

I/SLANDS

Maggie Harris

Discourse

You could try to reach me here
this island I have made my home
where one needs no passports
no struggling with language
where touchings of fingers on skin
stretches for the burn on bone

I'm sorry I mistook your name
'Narcissus', I called in my sleep
Apologies litter this passage of mine
like choral breaks in a litany
ships wrecked in the deep

Believing so much in the powers that lie
beneath the scent of new skin
hope took wing in democracies
grateful again and again

Always it is a You or an I
that craves less or more,
too late do I see that these marks on my palm
imprinted on that other shore
marked indelibly my ability to love
to mark trails

And yet I know (how I know!)
that no geography defines the land
as precisely as a heart.

So, you take my reticence for selfishness
Don't you know how far these travels

have already taken me?
And how wearing, how wearing they have been.

In the Stillness

your words launched like rocks
from the curve of your tongue
fall like pebbles on this limbless plane
where my fleshlessness waits

they scorch the space where skin had been
litter the starless skies
tumble in chasms
loose of the gravity which propelled them

in this stillness
stone meets stone
reflects stone
deflects stone

in this stillness
where the i
that you don't see
resides

stillness cups me into its centre
welcomes
no echo
no breeze
no sigh
only the limitless falling of matter

Waiting

He'll be in a good mood tonight
I know he will
I know he will

See, the table's laid all nice
He'll be pleased
Yes he'll be pleased

I've made his favourite pie for tea
He'll notice that
He'll notice that

Perhaps he'll only have had a pint
He used to once
He used to once

Later, in bed, I'll please him, see
Could be his Baby
His Baby yes

Only Baby's bottom gets punished then
Not Baby's arms
Or Baby's legs, no

He'll be in a good mood tonight
I know he will
I know he will

Communion

My white virginal
sacramental self
rises above you

Here i am your Host
your Eucharist
your U
your new Christ

my winged feet
dance upon your altar
this temple you created
out of Babylon.

You have bleached,
completely extinguished
my shadow

so we float, leukemic
while our marrow procreates,
propagates,
waits.

G'wan

So g'wan
ease out the door
don't wase yuh time shufflin yuh foot
like something stick pon the bottom

G'wan
ease out mih sight
don't wase yuh time jugglin yuh pocket
weighin whuh God know ain't dere

He watch yuh, yuh know
when yuh pump up pump up
an hang out the lace
God know how yuh an trip pon the road!

So g'wan, ease out mih sight
dem right when they say
don't marry big belly
big belly gon stand in yuh way

So move
ease out mih sight
with yuh shave head Armani
Nike and gears L.A.

we gon do
we be fine when he grow up
and turn tall and wise and wicked
jus like you

Orlando's Door

your children
and my children
press their faces to the glass of the garden door
whilst we, hours after lunch
still sip chateauneuf
 remembering

long summers past
at Knebworth
belly-up kissing the sky
Pink Floyd plucking chords right out of heaven
whilst we dragged on borrowed joints
rolled by men

you drank pints
even then
pre-supposing the revolution
whilst my scarlet-tipped nails
poured cider into glasses
pretending

now, watching you
curl like a cat
your arms coiled on the back of my sofa
it is moments like these when your eyes meet mine
that my toes curl up into my soft court shoes
and I hover, at Orlando's door.

Alternative Love Poem

Is it you, or the idea of you?
Is it those edges that frame your world
I am compelled to brush against,
To want against all wants, to enter?

If it is you then I can laugh
And remember touching you at last
After all this time of watching
When my fingers fanned the edges of your hairline
And breast to breast we danced.

If it is you I can smile
For you are so easy to love
With your cool calm stride
Your silences that speak volumes
The small tokens that you press
Time and again into my hand.

If it is you then I can relax
For no-one can take this away
This easy indulgence of falling
These slow fires we never fanned
This island whose edges cut away
Into a wild, blue sea.

If, however, it's the idea of you
That sends me reeling with alternatives
Then I seriously
Am in very deep shit.

Cocoon

So, Sister, the time has come
to re-weave my cocoon
re-immerse this embryonic self
this filament,
that had almost grown to reach you

I had grown webbed feet to swim
swum near to drowning
a nineties flapper, a mer-person on cobbles
that one perched on the pool table
in the lilac mesh dress

I must have lost the art of flirting
read nonchalance for intent -
Men are easy, they don't weave as we do
with blood for stitches. My mind flew fast before me,
making patterns.

Well they always said I ran before I walked.
I should have scanned the frontierland more closely
your ground within it,
known my crossing needed more than my needing of
you.

So it's back to the spinning
in this warm dark world
with the soft burr of voices like mine.
See here where I pricked my thumb,
the blood browning?
It fossilised quickly, seeking a swift death
bored with the slow weaving of my fingers.

Poem

Do you remember dragonflies?
And still water?
And a prince in a small white castle in the grounds?

Then let me leave clues
like Gretel's crumbs soon devoured
as she beat on edible doors
wearing one shoe, a ripped ballgown
and a sword strapped high on one thigh.

No?
Then try oaked casks, hops, doors

to gardens where Hansel leaned
against every tree trunk dressed in full combat gear.

You knew the name of every rose
but Gret's wisdom lay in trading crumbs for stones
engaging the aid of one fat frog
who bleat his little heart out by the stream.

Still no? Then remember dragonflies
who skim streams, still and yet hovering
little hearts pumping
like my small fists at your door.

For Miriam

they looked in my eyes for signs of tears
calling as they had, to tell me you had died

their arms hung at their sides
loose, palms at the ready to rise
stroke, calm the news away

instead
before the horror
before the numbing
before the wild cry
torn from a mind too dumb
to understand

you came to dance between us
where the sunlight hit the walls
lifting your Moroccan skirt
to improvise flamenco, rap and funk
and only when you placed your fingers to your lips
and winked

did the greyness of the walls close in
the shadows lifting off
to settle in between us

Misecho

Beyond the anger, confusion
Words like slingshots, fly
Taut, tight, controlled

Then loose and wild
Laying bare
A beating heart
Fragile and afraid

Remember

Remember turning the doorknob
slowly, clutching your artwork underarm
and entering, doe-eyed
a room full of strangers?

Remember him, turning sharp-eyed
you hanging your raincoat on the door
the blank sheet of paper
staring, cold, nude and bare?

His scent over your shoulders
his fingers aiming the charcoal
crumbling like you
a peppermint flutter of breath ...?

Remember, remember!
That first special night and then more

throwing gauntlets down
and placing the fingers at his door.

Remember curling like a cat
as he stroked
your work, your youth, your venus-flytrap-mind
you.

And then you -
converting his ears to Bob Marley
laughing his classicals away
puncturing his breath with tales
of disco queens and rap kings,
otherworlds of knowing.

That total immersion
that drawing between those worlds
where Dali and Beardsley both fell
that sharp-edged life where art becomes life becomes
art becomes hell.

Remember. Remember
the word love briefly appearing one day
smudged,
on Ingres paper.

PLATEAUX

Flying

in my indigo sleep i fly
wearing one large blue eye
its amber aureole rotates
becomes a telescope
watching the causeway ripple
beneath a deep blue sea

Solomon's Wisdom

Solomon, wise in the ways of the world
come settle this thing for a confuse woman
they spitting out thing about 'repatriate'
shoving all o' we through the departure gate

Man this thing it spinning in mih head
making mih so dizzy like I fall down dead
you see, I is an assembalation:
mih one foot white, the nother one brown
mih two eyes blue, and mih belly-button colour is
vermilion

You see Solomon mih old grandad he own plantation
mih old granma she work plantation
she, black as the night, he kinda off-white
while we chilren range from ivory to brown

So I thinking hard about repatriate
wondering, which pieca me going to go through
which gate?
Mih one foot ready for go run to the sun
while the nother one say he ain leaving town!

Mih right hand hold on to the fatherland
while mih blue eye them ah roll to the motherland
So Solomon man, tell me whuh for do
this mix-up woman in front o' you

SOLOMON sighed and as he wiped his eye
he said:
I won't be able to help you BOYO they've asked
me to leave as well!

First Class Travel, Second Class Mate

Sitting on a train. Waiting, waiting
Summer sweat hugging Levis and Nikes
washing sand from seashore, tapping.
Young mum clapping baby on knee
telling the world of baby-change need
whispers conspiratorially:
what we gonna do if the ticket-collector's
waiting at the gate at Margate?

The steel wheels move, they shunt and glide
and baby bounced high on Levis smiles
to the rhythm and a fingertip jibe:
my sweet baby, momma's baby
jellybelly! jellybelly!
On a train ride.
First class travel, second class mate.

In an English bar where wine priced high
increases its wantable value
Saturday nite respectables clink their glasses
with gold rings shining bright,
and ivories polished and capped

A lawyer, proud, boasts loud of his Citroen
hey up and how she rises
ascending like desire at the touch of his clutch
hubcaps naked and bare
low-key, liberal street credibility

Daddy downmarket, decorating tales through
breadpudding mouthfulls ...
Wife playing Baby opens mouth like a beak
for a spoonful of Daddy's sweet ...
Decorating tales of the house in Provence
and beams, rustic and real.

> Wife-face rises up within my night
> eyes black and bright and the distant
> rumbling of railway sidings shifting
> their rolling stock of human fear
> huddled like cattle in another time
> and now; her wine-lined voice
> proclaiming the desire for a fascist state
> and a party she could vote for.

But off we go - Jellybelly Jellybelly! On a train ride!
And the ticket collector straightens his cap
as the train pulls into the station.

Maggie Harris

My Latest Messenger

My latest messenger
flew in on a broomstick
dusted down her cords and leather
and emitted words of wisdom from her dark labyrinth
where turquoise-stippled feathers
gathered dust in corners.

"A good poet," she screeched
"does not exist what does not know
about thingies like trochies
and perambulitic metre!
What passes these days for poetry
is merely excuse for repartee!"

My messenger, who at first
I did not recognise
tormented me with whips of scorn
and I, forlorn, began to squirm
at such great crueltee

This poetself who once had yawned
through the Lord's Chillon
whose soul had sunk with the albatross
and woke with Len's *Suzanne*
had strutted its nouveau confidence
been blase on structure and form
 now it slithered its unbelieving self
into the womb coils of the mother's labyrinth

but then, the tongue of the serpent rose
ran licking along my spine

flamed up in the tum te tum
the clap hand foot down bum de bum
of a lickle thing call riddum

it shake itself remembering
how a poem can
mimic the pace of a pulse
race like the beat of a running heart
rip arteries to shreds

it shake itself remembering
how the lilt from the tilt of a golden tongue
can raise the hairs off skin and drip
like dew into the vein

so I strolled out cool in the sunshine
out of that dark labyrinth
just pausing to pluck one turquoise feather
and set it in my hair.

Lilies for the Martini Girl

There there.
Rest easy now, rest easy.

See the care I've taken (not took)
See me khaki-cool and clipped
and you equipped
linen suit new
and white
just the way
you like it.

See, I fold up your Massa-smooth hands
neat, across your chest
and the lilies
arrange like Jesus' halo
round you blue-eyed face.

Lilies for the Martini girl, you'd said
emptying your buttonhole
of its worship
and laying it lip up
amongst the dollar bills
and coca-cola spills
my rollerskates had trailed between the tables.

Rest easy now, rest easy.
Yuh know, a struggle sometime take four hundred
years.

And
it's not that I don't appreciate
your loving
your raising me from roller skates to high heel shoes
to Mandingo Apartment.
For this Sylvie-Baby learn to suck, blow
and handle percolator.
Sylvie-Baby learn to cool her dressing down
for Massa Daddy.

No, it's not that I don't appreciate what you done for
me.
Enough is enough is all
no amount o' perfume nor holy water
won't wash tar babies clean.

So rest easy, rest easy there.

Lilies from the Martini girl
just match the colour of your hair.

They Said

They said, you're a woman now
when the blood ran down
but no-one told me why

they said, you're a woman now
and they waved goodbye
as i climbed high
in an english plane seeking other womankind

they laughed and crossed their legs
stocking-smooth and stillettoed
while i, bare-legged and open-toed
mis-matched handbags
and waited
on dance floors

they said, you're a woman now
and wiped their eyes as i
beautifully wandered up and then back down
the aisle

they said, you're a woman now
when seeking sisterhood i told
of the wedding night spent crawling
off a brand new bedroom floor

they said, you're a woman now
and women have to give it
on demand

they said, you're a woman now
when my baby smiled her angel smile
and that my floating feeling
was only pethidine

But there was no-one to re-affirm
this fact of womanhood
when the slap that called me whore
slammed my head against the door
for daring to look for love
outside the bedroom door

no-one to confirm
this fact of womanhood
when i gathered up my children
and took them from the fold

no-one to re-affirm
this paradigm of woman
'till i grabbed their condemnation
piled it up like bricks

stackpiled this affirmation:
Me. New. Womankind.
I.

Portrait of a Woman Artist

image and illusion
i am dancing in the sun
they are watching from the shade
lifting their daiquiris with a smile
and a once-crisp Panama hat
curling in the heat

tenders simmering displeasure
at the rash impropriety
of white skinned children
dancing in the sun.

image and illusion
i am living by the sea
i am running from the questions
i am dancing on the flint
and my breath on the wing
and my print on the tideline
rash impropriety
naked naked me.

image and illusion
he has paused to feel my rhythm
he is seeking his reflection
he is looking at Madonna, at his mother
at every slack-thighed woman
smiling down from a bookshelf
but i'm pleasing
with my barefeet on the rocks
imprinting my image
tango tango

searching for the language
i am weaving it with hessian
i am moulding it with clay

searching for the language
i'm imprinting my image
tango tango

tango you tango me
i am happyhappyhappy

with my big white smile and pockets full
of sand
and daiquiris
and lost mommas
and blackberries in a pie
but this is MY picture
see?

Collection

you can stroke me if you like
with your knuckled fingers
crooked and eager to smooth
this *trompe l'oeil* barely breathing above you
veins threaded like the very best of cheeses
or bluest of marble

a succession of others have placed me here
with enough room to swivel to my heart's content
believing my spaces to be ungendered and limitless

stroke away then
think of alabaster and magnificent tombs
of warrior archangels with chests instead of breasts
but with still-beating hearts
left bleeding on worn copper plates.

Other

bring me to the light fantastic
i am neither young nor white
and still in the process of belonging

but here i stand anyway
crisp at edges, soft at centre
more september than june
more toffee than pineapple
and bristling with brown sugar cubes

i am that statistic,
that other

Cocktail

my alter ego dressed for dinner
smart in black and baby diamonds
pasted to one ear

tables wilting, haute couture
Carmen's daughter cha cha cha-ing
burning rosette mango lips
of effigies of cygnets cut in ice

her sister flows beneath her skin
a coffee silhouette
a ready-mixed cocktail

Phrases

"Fucking wog".
Shadow ghosting bedroom in Ramsgate.

"She lika gole hair dolly eh?"
East indian children on the Corentyne.

"Devil child!"
Grandfather confiscating radio in New Amsterdam.

"Fuckin ate white wogs fuckin do".
Propping up the bar in Deal.

"You ain't a man till you fuck a tan".
Songster on the train to Canterbury.

"Fucking Pakis. Fucking Blacks. I'm up to 'ere wi'it.
I tell you. Fucking shit. Gimme a fucking drink in
this fucking bar.
I'm fucking parched, I tell you".
Pub in Whitstable.

So my children/
women of colour/white/black/mixed race/colored/
afro-saxon
phrases or whole sentences?

candlelight!
candlelight of the human race
candlelight!

Women Writers Tour, Muze 1997

Yet to be unpacked
suitcase on the bedroom floor lies open
clothes folded, resigned now to travel
and a permanent impermanence of mind.
Poet circles
will unpack soon, lay the empty case
on lip of waiting wardrobe
where its empty dark interior will fester

perpetuate stagnant midnight spaces
empty of Gallic voices raised in song.

Open, those voices roam
in a fritillary of language
the dry ash of a Gitane smoking its way
through husky-toned French folksong
the march of Tipperary
a Rumanian Clementine. The full body
of an Irish laugh bounds,
a lush vin de rouge, its lunchtime invocation
on Catholic lips fleshed with sinfulness.

Here a menu card, a Bruxelles map
flat between pajamas
nights wide-sheeted with loneliness tremble
like the tongue undressed
the naked poet-self desperate
for audience; clutching the stomach in fear
whilst reaching for stilletoes to dance like Salome
dance and tremble to, with, for language.

Dinner table. White linened, Midnight in Lille.
Stone walled ivory tower
hovers on winding stair. An almost First Supper
redolent in memory. Of union. Warm arms elbowing.
Waiters, white-robed supplicants
circle the edge of tables, heads bowed
hands cupping communions of coffee
in small white china cups.

The ghost of a fish knife lies silent
ambassador to fillets in roux, terrines
that never got eaten, victim
to the alien inhibition
of an almost-English tongue.

Poet circles
yes, will unpack soon
liberate a wistfulness of coherent
concrete, meaning.

Little Coloured Girl

Little COLOURed girl throw stone
throw stone
roll hit black water
lookie see lookie see
stone come back
fly back
hit
little coLOURed girl shouldn't throw stone

Little CoLOuRed girl blow leaf
blow leaf
fly fall Papaground
lookie see lookie see
leaf come back
fly back
hit
little colOURED girl shouldn't blow leaf

Little colOured girl roll bead
roll bead
spin twist blue eye
lookie see lookie see
bead come back
spin back
hit
little COlouRed girl shouldn't roll bead

Little ColoUred girl start dance
no shoes
foot slap Papaground
lookie see lookie see
foot them a fly
hand wild
eyea spin
hand clap meka see yuh Chakari
dance mih girlchile
dance dANCE DANCE!

Lala

ah Lala! when i returned
there you were, too soon
running down Main Street
with the knife in your hand
and curlers in your hair

no time! no time! you cried
your cheeks white
where anger had long since
crystallized
your tears and fear

had long since tensed
those palms
that once had rolled mudpies
and bushcooked callaloo
beneath the stairs

now you run from bar to bar
looking for your man
who whispers promises

and drips legacies
into other women's bellies

Lala! Lala!
perhaps
we should have had gunfights instead
pistols in our yard
instead of rolling rotis
and scolding dolls
whose heads rolled vacuously
from side to side

Girlchild

Chakari could tell a mango from a guinep
a soursop from an okra
a star-apple from same
she could suck tamarind sweet from ripe
or green and hot with birdpepper
she could tell you who The Hermits were
and who was in America Hit Parade
what wet-look boots were
and who had just come back from abroad

but she couldn't tell you where wild tamarind grew
or how to propagate them
she couldn't tell you what the season was for
starapples
or how long it took for hibiscus-cheese-and-bread
to grow
her ears rang with the sound of church bells
rang with don't don't don't
rang with jangles from Radio Parimaribo
Fab 208 pop posters that spoke
nose wrinkled with the smell of new books

when asked some decades later
of the totality of knowledge
her offguard answer ran:
only the wild and the sinful,
never girlchildren, ran barefoot on the backdam.

Running Woman

She ran out into the streets
Catalena from Potaro Falls
'bused up by some husband hungry with his fists
thirsty with rum, mad with the smell of some dorado
and the memory of red ants and mosquitoes

Only this is Margate and I must be dreaming
see my country sister run, fight and bite
dragged off this quiet street by a policeman

The job was tidy, she had said
and I am wicked! I am fine!
But she embraced the upholstery of pubs
held them close to her bosom
wore mini-skirts past forty
and sang Sparrow calypsos even though
they were most inappropriate to woman.

Catalena had managed to escape
cross-country from fists to getting pissed
into a freedom cross-referenced
by brutality, hopes of immortality
plateaux-space created
by her swift and constant running

Now her voice bounds like waterfalls, stretch-limos
hunting dogs, howler monkeys:

If I had the wings I could fly
If I had the wings I could fly
and dodoorunrunrundodoorunruffflyawayflyaway ...
and away and away ...

Scratching in the Fowlyard

Aisla is flying in her highrise flat
staring at the sea through clear window-panes
floating her arms on the UPVC sill
echoing her veins in red railings and pipes
a Pompidou Centre in Margate

Aisla is stacked like a cube in breeze-block
Demerara sugarcube, crumbling, dissolving
wedged like elastic on the 23rd floor
where the lift glides and rolls
and shudders on tubings of plastic

Aisla is dreaming of chickens and yards
where the mesh fence has fallen
the pickets are flat
and Rhode Island Reds peck at tamarind seeds
who lie where the mighty have fallen

But this, this, this fowlyard, this ...
exists in a pocket of air
and her fingernails rake at sheer panes of glass
at herring-gulls tilting on salt-water wings
Kings of the highrise
Cocks of the air
Queens of the concrete promenades.

Thelma Dancing

Thelma danced. On Saturday nights fit to falling
On Saturday nights with the kids in bed
Thelma planned her dancing, quick
To the step and a flick of the wrist
The high heel shoes, the black frock
Hair curled to a turn, black mascara.

Thelma was a veggie
Protester for animal rights
The one with the mouth at Dover
Ten years earlier it woulda been Greenham but
Dover would suffice, she travelled light
And Saturday night was worth the fight

Throbbed enough in the flickering light
Passed the word, knock 'em dead while standing
In the frock with the peepsie hole
And the long, tight slit.
Bacardi Breezers, bottles of Woodies
Thelma hits the floor, shameless, alone

The dancing was hers alone

All the shamin and the carin
The kids, the men, now the veal calves
Floated to the wall while she hit the floor
Smashing her way through Massive Attack
Mooning through the Titanic tune
Stitching the week, fuelling her feet
Seaming the space between bars/plateaux/astral horizons

Thelma dancing
Dancing fit to falling
On a Saturday night with the kids in bed
And nothing but the dance in her head.

For the Snow Queen
(somewhere in Antarctica)

So that's where she landed!
I'd often looked out in second-hand bookshops
thumbed through those early written tales
in which the tongue was stolen, captured
stitched within the pages, dressed for sale.
I'd even pored through Swedish phone books
Swedish ones, Norwegian ones
thumbing through such a list of Andersens my dear,
you've no idea.

I was giving up, I tell you
getting to the point when, after reading Hillman
I began to recreate this archetype
my twentieth-century angel
goddess of the now, my mirrored one
projected of the me-that-was
sad shit, you know.
I'd even learned to paint. I painted her
ice-clad of course, in simply-gorgeous bluesand greens
wherein reflected snow; quite similar aesthetically
to that well known Other
in her mantled skyblue and don't forget the halo.

But Snowy now, she always was more my cup of tea
though it bothered me sometimes, the attraction
When I was six I thought her wicked
when wicked meant wicked not cool

and cried for Kay and worshipped Gerd
my heroine, my jewel.
But I soon erased that wimpy Kay, shoved Gerd off the
mountain,
painted Me in. On the canvas Me and Her stand posing
photocall time, real root sisters, ice, man
specially when I added that cerulean blue.

Now just when I thought I'd sorted things
accepted day is day, night is night
and no amount of sponsored walks will save the Yamomani

here's the news, front page -
nearly smacked me in the face -
You've resurfaced way down South
beneath Antarctica, refashioned your ice palace
in that last safe place where the Russkies
and the Japanese and Scientese-Amerikies play Niceties
and promisepromisePromise
to keep their filthy hands off your skis.

Well it's left me in a right dilemma.
Shall I dig out those crampons I'd ordered for Alaska
head to
save my Sister, be a
Rainbow Warrior, a truly
Ecobabe?
See the thing is Snowy, Hillman's right
I've got the nigglingest of feelings it's too late for you and
me
like, my archetypes have shifted, shoved around a bit
and like, there's another Sister waiting in the wings
so though it might be tempting fate with all that
global warming stuff, all I can say at this late stage
is
stay cool Sis, hold the page.

Maggie Harris

Last-Year-Dolly Writes a Letter

Well dear Chakari,

i got your news about your coming visit
what a turn-up for the books!

well is about time yuh remembuh me
yuh pack up and gone so fast
yuh never seh goodbye
ah nevah even see a drop 'o water in yuh eye

before yuh cyan seh JesusMaryJoseph
yuh fly pass, yuh fly out, yuh gone
yuh lef yuh cyat yuh dog dih bicycle yuh friens
even dih coolie boyfren
and yuh lef me

yuh tek she doh, that flypass kissmeass
Barbie dolly who waltz in here one Chrismuss
and nevuh lef, tek up residence
like some govment house jenny

yuh tek she hole onto she
wearing dih fancy dress yuh mek she
on yuh granny machine up Kwakwani
an year after year in dat Englun
is she yuh stick pon top yuh Chrismuss tree

but i know she wasn't no angel
she was (God forgive me) a slut
small enough to fit in yuh case
but big enough to flaunt her butt
back to whey she came from in the furse place

Limbolands

i know i was jus hard plastic and rags
mih one eye drop out long since
the nailpolish yuh paint on mih flake off
mih nice hair frizzup in the sun

yes i know i wasn't no beauty
but nevah mind, i know yuh still love me
even doh yuh nevuh sew me no new dress like slutbarbie
cos yuh seh i too big

but yuh still coulda find me a teeny place
in that big brown suitcase
after all, yuh tek yuh daddy guitar
an yuh cyant even play he

and as for dem two bigass American dolly
dem gone too, sit up pon yuh sister lap
pon the aeroplane smilin like some doolally
tomfool who lost they call

but ah seh, don't mind don't mind
nevuh mind slutbarbie, the guitar
nor dem Yankeedoodledollie
squatting like jackass pon yuh desk
cross all o' dat water

i know is me ME ME yuh always love the best

so i excited and i waiting till i see yuh soon
my faraway mommy
lovyaeveranever xxx
 last-year-dolly (andrea)

ps: when yuh comin please to fetch me a new dress.
anything in lime green will do.
xxx L.Y.D.

Steelpan Armadillo Girl

you may be there tonight watching me
remembering our intimacies
my face upturned in the rain
catching its falling in a hungry throat

you may be there tonight watching me
rocking in the power of memory
remembering how you rolled me in your palm
and i let you so willingly
so gratefull to be there, little mudpie girl
loving your fat thumbs
your cradling
foolishly, foolishly loving you

you may be there tonight watching me
but i an no mudpie girl no more
o no koloka no koloka not me

i've grown into a steelpan girl
an armadillo me
armadillo close to the ground
steelpan breastplate longing for the minute when it rain
an the rain beatin riddum pon de plate

you think you cyan break me?
o no koloka no koloka not me

you may be there tonight watching me
remembering some little mudpie girl
who lied that she loved you one sad time
and you rolled her soft belly

up on the plains
and left her there to dry

you think you cyan break me?
o no koloka no koloka not me
not me

A Scattering of Tongues

scattered like seeds
borne on wings
carried on the soles of feet

floating on water
trickling fish rasping breath
from dry riverbeds

we remember these marks of our passage
strange earth, hardened footbottoms
that no-one came to greet us
singing the songs of home

we remember the tapping in darkness
whispers from the darkness
growing like seeds in the darkness
learning new morse codes

we watched and listened
reached for the light
now on land and water, train and boat
house/towerblock
songbirds are waking
songbirds are waking!
from these dark quiet tunnels of our throats

Babel

Here, I will feed you goats milk and rock you in the cradle
of my imaginings
I will loosen all fastenings, buttonings, shoe lacings, release
you to roll unencumbered in pillows of sand, settle your
small feet in rockpools.

Here, I will christen this large rock my own.
Watch while you engineer your flight path through tangles
of fish lines and seaweed which sluggishly, elegantly frames
the wet chalk like hair.

These are the tongues you will speak:
That crab marching full steam past his lamp-posts of coke-
cans
full-steam up his driveway of driftwood.
The historylessness of that solitary footprint marooned on
a slither of sand.
This swift come to rest in baptismal oil.
This tortoiseshell hairslide. This remnant of rope.

Do not look back to the promenade where Gomorrans are
clicking in a Babel of concrete.
Here in the soft shades of wingspans and tumultuous
screechings of gulls, these will soon fade to a whispering,
drown at the turn of the tide.

Here. This is where we must begin:
by tracing these patterns on a damp mussel shell with
fingertips oiled and prepared.
By laying our heads on the damp sand beside it.
By placing its lips to our ear.

OTHER TITLES
FROM
MANGO PUBLISHING

Leaves in the Wind *Selected Writings of Beryl Gilroy*
£12.99 (ISBN 1 902294 00 9)

Haunted by History *Poetry by Joan Anim-Addo*
£6.99 (ISBN 1 902294 03 3)

Another Doorway: Visible Inside the Museum
Poetry and Short Stories from the Caribbean Women Writers' Alliance
£6.00 (ISBN 1 902294 01 7)

Voice Memory Ashes: Lest We Forget
Poetry and Short Stories Celebrating and Paying Homage
to the Collective Memory of Caribbean Experience
£6.00 (ISBN 1 902294 04 1)

A Way to Catch the Dust *Short Stories by Jacob Ross*
£8.99 (ISBN 1 902294 08 4)

Windrush to Lewisham: 'Memoirs of Uncle George'
by W. George Brown
£6.00 (ISBN 1 902294 07 6)

Mango Publishing
PO Box 13378, London SE27 0ZN

108